When Wilma Rudolph Played BASKETBALL

by Mark Weakland

illustrated by Daniel Duncan

PICTURE WINDOW BOOKS
a capstone imprint

During the 1960 Olympic Games in Rome, Italy, a young woman took her place next to the other runners at the starting line. The gun fired with a POP! Wilma Rudolph, a runner from the United States, surged forward. She was all power and fluid motion.

Eleven seconds later Wilma crossed the finish line first. She had won the gold medal in the women's 100-meter dash.

It was the moment Wilma had imagined. She was no longer the sickest girl in Clarksville, Tennessee. She was the fastest woman in the world!

Wilma Rudolph was born, June 23, 1940. She was the 20th child in a family of 22 children. Because she was born almost two months early, Wilma was a tiny baby. She weighed just a little more than 4 pounds (1.81 kilograms).

Wilma's parents didn't know then that Wilma would one day become famous.

Wilma was an energetic baby. But her early birth caused health problems. Wilma became sickly after her first year. By the time she was 4 years old, she had suffered through chicken pox, pneumonia, whooping cough, and scarlet fever.

In the 1940s racial discrimination made it hard for black people to get good medical care. So Wilma's mother cared for her at home. She piled on blankets and made hot drinks to help cure Wilma's illnesses.

Wilma complained about her mother's remedies. "All these blankets make me sweat," she said. "And your medicine tastes awful!"

Wilma eventually recovered from her illnesses. But something else was wrong. Wilma's mother took her to the doctor.

After finishing his examination, the doctor spoke to Wilma's mother. "I'm sorry, Blanche," he said. "Your daughter has polio."

The polio left Wilma's leg crooked and her foot turned inward.
The doctor told them Wilma needed a leg brace.

"The doctor says you won't walk without that brace, Wilma,"
said her mother. "But I know you will."

"I believe you, Momma," said Wilma.

Twice a week Wilma and her mother took a bus to a medical college 50 miles (80.5 kilometers) away. There, Wilma received physical therapy for her leg.

Spending so much time trying to get well was tough on Wilma. She couldn't play with other children. By the time she was 7 years old, Wilma was fed up, but she was also determined.

"No more taking what comes ... Enough is enough."

Wilma imagined herself walking and running without her brace.
Most importantly, Wilma followed her imagination with action. She
did exercises. She took off her brace, and she practiced walking without it.

"I'm going to be healthy just like the rest of them," she said to herself.

Soon Wilma could walk well enough to go to school.
"Finally," she said. "A place I can be with other kids."

As she grew older, Wilma realized how difficult life was for most African Americans. She saw racial discrimination everywhere.

Segregation meant that black people couldn't do the same things as white people. They had to use separate drinking fountains and bathrooms. They even had to sit at the backs of buses.

Wilma also noticed how hard her own mother worked as a maid and cook.

"There's something not right about all this," Wilma thought. "White folks got all the luxury, and we black folks got the dirty work." Wilma became determined to do something other than serve white people.

At age 9 Wilma took a huge step forward. One Sunday Wilma's parents held open the church door for her, as they always had.

"Hold on," Wilma said. "There's something I have to do."

Wilma took off her brace outside. Then she propped her crutches against the wall, opened the door, and walked inside. Wilma limped down the aisle. People watched as she walked by. One woman even yelled out. Wilma beamed and kept on walking.

By the time she was 12 years old, Wilma's brace was off for good. For years she had watched other children play on the playground. She had studied girls playing basketball and memorized their moves. Now she was determined to be on the basketball team.

She thought to herself, "**Wilma, tomorrow ... tomorrow you're going to see what it feels like to play a little basketball.**"

Wilma signed up for the basketball team. But for the first few years, she didn't get much playing time. Coach C.C. Gray only put her in at the end of a game, when her team was sure to win, or sure to lose.

But Wilma was determined. She practiced hard, sometimes for hours a day. Coach Gray jokingly called her Skeeter. **"You're little, you're fast and you always get in my way!"** he said.

Before her fourth season, Wilma continued buzzing like a "skeeter." **"Coach Gray,"** she said. **"... if you put as much time on me as you do on some of these other girls, I'd be a star player on this team."**

Her persistence paid off. Right before the first game that year, Coach Gray put Wilma in as a guard.

Burt High School, Wilma's team, hosted a tournament that season. During one game Wilma scored 32 points! And Burt High had a new star—Wilma Rudolph.

Wilma was a star basketball player, but her best talent was running.

"I love the feeling of freedom in running," she said.

When Ed Temple, the track coach at Tennessee State University, saw Wilma playing basketball, he was impressed. She was a small teenager, but she had amazing speed and focus. Coach Temple invited Wilma to join his sports training camp. There she trained with the university's women's track club, The Tigerbelles.

The Tigerbelles were already famous for winning Olympic medals in 1952. Wilma would add to their fame. While in high school, she ran with them in the 1956 Olympic games. The USA's four-woman relay team was made up of Wilma and three other Tigerbelles. Together the women earned a bronze medal in the relay race.

Now that she had a taste of victory, Wilma was determined to do better. She wanted to be standing on the gold medal platform at the next Olympic Games. Four years later she achieved that goal.

Afterword

Wilma's greatest accomplishment came at the 1960 Olympic Games in Rome. First was the 100-meter dash. No one could beat her blazing speed. Wilma ran away with her first Olympic gold medal.

Next came the 200-meter dash. The crowd in the stadium knew of Wilma's recent win. Now they were rooting for her. "Wil-ma, Wil-ma, Wil-ma!" they chanted.

The starting pistol fired and Wilma leaped forward. Twenty-four seconds later, she crossed the finish line. She had won a second gold medal!

Wilma also ran the last leg of the 400-meter relay race, and the U.S. team won. The Olympic crowd went wild. Wilma Rudolph was the first American woman to win three gold medals in track and field in a single Olympics. Once unable to walk without crutches, Wilma was now "the fastest woman in the world." She was also quite famous.

Wilma retired from her track career in 1962. She became a teacher, a high school coach, a mother to four children, and even a fashion model. She died at age 54 of a brain tumor.

Wilma was an inspiration to thousands of athletes, especially young women. She taught young people everywhere that even when the odds seem to be against them, they can achieve great things.

Glossary

brace—a device that clamps things tightly together

discrimination—treatment in favor of or against

inspiration—a person who inspires or positively influences

luxury—high quality materials; riches

persistence—the act of keeping at something; staying the course

polio—a virus that affects the nerves, especially those that control muscles

racial—having to do with a person's race, or the major group in which humans can be divided; people of the same race share a physical appearance, such as skin color

relay—a race in which teammates run part of a distance

segregation—setting people apart; keeping people in a separate group

Read More

Goddu, Krystyna Poray. *What's Your Story, Wilma Rudolph?* Minneapolis: Lerner Publications, 2016.

McCann, Michelle Roehm. *Girls Who Rocked the World: Heroines from Joan of Arc to Mother Teresa.* New York: Aladdin/Beyond Words, 2012.

Wade, Mary Dodson. *Amazing Olympic Athlete Wilma Rudolph.* Amazing Americans. Berkeley Heights, N.J.: Enslow Publishers, 2010.

Critical Thinking With the Common Core

1. What particular character traits did Wilma Rudolph exhibit as a young person and how did these traits help her to accomplish her goals? Provide two examples and support your answer with words from the text. (Key Ideas and Details)

2. Did the adults in Wilma Rudolph's life try to help her become an active and independent person, or did they try to stop her from becoming an active and independent person? Support your answer with two pieces of evidence from the text. (Integration of Knowledge and Ideas)

3. The author wrote, "Wilma taught young people that even when the odds seem to be against them, they can achieve great things." What evidence in the book supports this statement? Provide two examples. (Craft and Structure)

Internet Sites

FactHound offers a safe, fun way to find Internet sites related to this book. All of the sites on FactHound have been researched by our staff.

Here's all you do:

Visit *www.facthound.com*

Type in this code: 9781479596843

Super-cool stuff! Check out projects, games and lots more at **www.capstonekids.com**

Other Titles in this Series

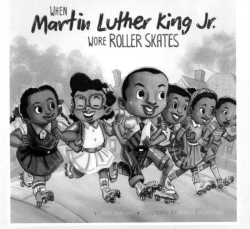

Index

Special thanks to our adviser for her advice and expertise:
Maureen M. Smith Ph.D., California State University, Sacramento
Department of Kinesiology and Health Science

Editor: Shelly Lyons
Designer: Ashlee Suker
Creative Director: Nathan Gassman
Production Specialist: Tori Abraham
The illustrations in this book were created digitally.

Editor's Note: Direct quotations are indicated by **bold** words.

Direct quotations are found on the following pages:
page 10, line 6: Rudolph, Wilma.
Wilma: The Story of Wilma Rudolph.
New York: Signet, 1977, page 19.

page 15, lines 1 and 3: Ibid., page 8.

page 18, line 5: Ibid., page 39.

page 20, line 5: Roberts, M.B. "Rudolph Ran and
World Went Wild," ESPN.com.
https://espn.go.com/sportscentury/features/00016444.html

page 23, line 2: Rudolph, Wilma.
Wilma: The Story of Wilma Rudolph.
New York: Signet, 1977 pages 47–48.

page 24, line 2, Ibid., page 50.

Picture Window Books are published by Capstone,
1710 Roe Crest Drive, North Mankato, Minnesota 56003
www.mycapstone.com

Library of Congress Cataloging-in-Publication Data
Cataloging-in-publication information is on file with the Library of
Congress. Written by Mark Weakland.
ISBN 978-1-4795-9684-3 (library hardcover)
ISBN 978-1-5158-0136-8 (paperback)
ISBN 978-1-5158-0144-3 (eBook PDF)

Printed in the United States   5664